Pisces

February 20 — March 20

Thru the Numbers

Pisces
February 20 — March 20

by
Paul & Valeta Rice

SAMUEL WEISER, INC.

York Beach, Maine

First published in 1983 by
Samuel Weiser, Inc.
Box 612
York Beach, Maine 03910

Reprinted, 1991

Library of Congress Catalog Card Number: 82-63004

ISBN 0-87728-576-4 (Pisces)

BJ

Printed in the United States of America

Depending on the year involved, the sun changes
zodiac signs on different days, consequently sources
vary in the dates they give to indicate the change-
over. Those born close to the beginning/end of a
sign are not on the "cusp" as is commonly believed.
There is a clear demarcation. If you are unsure of
your sign you may want to have your chart
calculated—or you can buy both books and see
which one works for you!

Contents

AUTHORS

If Valeta and Paul Rice sound familiar, it may be because of their extensive travel around the United States, from Alaska to the coast of California, from the East coast to Hawaii. During their invitational stopovers, they conducted workshops and seminars about Name Analysis and Birth Analysis. This continued for over twenty years until Paul's death in 1988.

Paul Rice was an engineer and Valeta a minister and psychic counselor. While their professions were very different they shared an interest in occult studies for more than 40 years, which started with their introduction to a book about ESP from Duke University. Their search for esoteric knowledge carried them into astrology, reincarnation, palmistry, tarot, color, music, I Ching, ESP, dream analysis, the qabala, yoga, structural dynamics, meditation/visualization/healing and many more sciences—techniques found both beneficial and rewarding by their clients.

They have also published *Potential: The Name Analysis Book* (Samuel Weiser, 1987) which provides an in-depth look at the special numerological nuances your name holds.

Valeta Rice still holds private consultations and is also available for lectures. She can be contacted at:

Valeta Rice
F.A.C.E. Association
177 Webster Street, #A105
Monterey, CA 93940

WHEN?

When shall I start my next project?
When should I ask for a raise?
When should I sign that contract?
When should I get married?
How will I feel when I retire?

How many times has a person looked for an answer to these questions? During this modern age the veil has been lifted on the ancient science of the vibration of the NUMBERS. This ancient science, known as the *metaphysical science of numerology*, was developed by Pythagoras, who lived in the sixth century B.C.

The simplicity of NUMEROLOGY is astounding. If you can count on your fingers you can use Numerology. It requires only a few hours study before you can begin to put to use the basic facts that you have acquired. This knowledge will give one the opportunity to see himself and other acquaintances in a better light. Apparently its simplicity is the reason Numerology was used less than other occult sciences in the past, and our society today seems to prefer complexity also.

Surprisingly, the knowledge of the numbers which govern your life will reveal many things you already know, that you had suspected or you had hoped were true.

The Numerologist takes his place alongside the Astrologer, Graphologist, Palmist and the Tarot reader, who all believe that we came into this life, not by chance, but by choice, and from these arts or sciences much can be revealed about a person's life.

Numerology reveals the vibrations in many categories including the number connected to the Birth Date, the Personal Year, the Personal Month and how the planet vibrations correlate to these numbers.

The awareness of the numbers connected to these categories helps us with a yearly and monthly course to follow.

Everyone wants to be happy and prosperous. Many unfortunate people have not learned to harmonize their birthdate vibrations with the timing of their decisions.

We are constantly called upon to make decisions which may make significant changes in our lives. Often we make the wrong decisions over family, friends, or in business because our "TIMING" is off.

The simple system of the vibration of the numbers and how they pertain to your life and the timing of your decisions will help you to come to logically deduced insights and, if carefully followed,will make you increasingly happy and prosperous throughout your lifetime.

Pythagoras, who lived twenty-five centuries ago, is considered the Father of Numbers. It is believed that he received his knowledge of the occult value of the numbers while in Egypt and Babylon. He taught these concepts and many more in his School of Occult Philosophy where the few who were allowed to attend learned how "everything can be related to numbers."

The Science of Numerology is not a quick way to happiness and achievement; it is only by becoming aware of your favorable number vibrations and then changing the unfavorable vibrations that you can smooth your pathway.

Numbers live and numbers tell and everyone can become aware of their vibrations and their relationship to themselves through the numbers.

We have explored the mundane and esoteric values of the numbers and their relationship to astrology with a lot of help from our guides.

This knowledge we wish to share with you.

PISCES

February 20th to March 20th   MUTABLE/WATER

The FISHES   Ruler: NEPTUNE

Pisces, symbolized by the fishes swimming upstream and downstream at the same time, can be thought of as a person who has a hard time making up his mind. Or Pisces can be a person searching in the past and in the future for answers to his soul's quest.

This compassionate sign is the most sensitive in the Zodiac. Pisceans feel deeply, and woe betide the mate or lover who wounds their pride. Their moods swing from indifference to bitter sarcasm; from charm to irritation; from bewitchment to resentment—and not too slowly at that. Pisces would be more comfortable mated with a **4, 5, 7, 8,** or **9** because these numbers have calm, introspective and adventurous souls that will not trespass on the Piscean sensitivity without thinking about it first.

Many people call Pisces the scrap pile of the universe. Little bits and pieces of all the signs are stored in Pisces, which gives them an understanding of many different kinds of people. Pisces really doesn't want to be here—or there either. Pisces wants to be someplace else in the universe. They instinctively know there is a better place to be—somewhere.

The positive vibrations of this sign show a wisdom far beyond that of the average person. It seems Pisceans are tuned into some other planet that is far advanced over ours. We could call this psychic or clairvoyant ability, yet the Piscean is apt to negate this as being too mystical.

One thing is sure, don't try to cage a Piscean or put him into a position where the work space is 6 x 6 and he's chained to a desk. He seeks freedom to wander, like the fishes, taking his neat, clean and graceful self outdoors and into activities that give him space and peace.

Gentle, emotional, imaginative, dreamy, fearful and interesting Pisces loves security and gambles on it.

PARTNERS: Pisceans, being the dreamers of the Zodiac, can miss their greatest opportunities to make money, make love or make a move toward fame and recognition. When they do come to and realize it's time to get on with some sensible goal, they have no trouble at all gaining their objectives. There is another way out; marry for money, or, find an ambitious mate who just "loves" to work. Perhaps the two of you would prefer living "on the beach." You are the romantic one!

NEPTUNE: The great mask wearer! This sensitive planet, the ruler of Pisces, shows wisdom, intuitiveness, genius, and contact with other dimensions. The music Pisces enjoys is like falling water, poetic and graceful, producing visions of fantasy. Neptune sinks deeply into the sea trying to hide his intelligence behind the coral of obscurity and illusion. But a snap into reality will bring out the creativity and devotion that Neptune brings to this much maligned sign.

MUTABLE: Flexibility is the keyword, willingness to adapt to circumstances, tolerance and easy-goingness, sometimes prone to negativity, changeability and lack of will, or so it seems. This person can cope with nine grandchildren (all fussy eaters), an **8** Leo for a mate, three boy children who tower above this dainty little woman, and she handles them all—while they all think they are protecting her!

WATER: You would think with all this to-and-froing that Pisces is an unstable person—don't be fooled for they have compassion for the human race (unless they are totally negative characters) and understand the emotional upheavals that others have. They have been there and back and prefer to withdraw rather than fight, and they come out with fewer bruises.

NEGATIVE VIBRATIONS: Self-delusion, fearful, enjoying self-martyrdom, inertia and oversentimental.

NUMBER: The NUMBER that is connected to the Pisces BIRTH SIGN increases or decreases energy. Wherever you find Pisces in your chart look at the influence your DESTINY NUMBER has on this house in your horoscope.

HOW TO COMPUTE YOUR DESTINY

Your DESTINY, sometimes called the LIFE PATH, is the road that you as an individual travel. This is why you are here, what you should be doing in this lifetime in order to fulfill your soul. The NUMBER combined with your PISCES BIRTH SIGN reveals your soul urge, your reason for incarnating this lifetime. If you do not follow your DESTINY, you can become frustrated with unresolved goals.

Each month is represented by a number:

JANUARY	1	APRIL	4	JULY	7	OCTOBER	1
FEBRUARY	2	MAY	5	AUGUST	8	NOVEMBER	2
MARCH	3	JUNE	6	SEPTEMBER	9	DECEMBER	3

Write your BIRTHDATE on your PERSONAL CHART, page 26, using the NAME of your month—February or March—not the number of the month. Be sure to use the full year, i.e., 1935, NOT '35; or 1940, NOT '40, or whatever is the year of your birth. We use the "1" in the year, i.e., 1935, 1966, 1940, as well as the rest of the numbers.

On scratch paper add the number of the month, the day of the month and the year of your birth together; then reduce this number by constantly adding the numbers together until you come to a single digit or a MASTER NUMBER.

The MASTER NUMBERS are **11, 22, 33, 44, 55** and **66.**

EXAMPLE: Feb.   23,   1942$(1 + 9 + 4 + 2 = 16, 1 + 6 = 7)$
            2   5   7 $= 14; 1 + 4 =$ **5**
EXAMPLE: March 13,   1932
            3   13   6 $=$ **22, or 4**
EXAMPLE: March 12,   1935
            3   12   18 $=$ **33, or 6**

By trying different combinations of the numbers you can find "hidden" MASTER NUMBERS. Even though we do find the Master Numbers we always write the final result as **11/2, 22/4, 33/6, 44/8, 55/1** and **66/3.**

We call these last two examples *Research and Discovery* since we have found a *hidden* Master Number. When the Master Numbers are hidden an unexpected talent lies in the direction of the vibration of that particular number.

EXAMPLE: March 13, 1932 = 3 + 1 + 3 + 1 + 9 + 3 + 2 = **22.**
EXAMPLE: 3 + 4 + 6   = 13; 1 + 3 = **4**

So, Pisces, every time you find a **1, 2, 4, 6** or **8** in your birth sign or someone else's birth sign try all these methods. Then you find out if you or another person is vibrating on the Master Number or the single digit. There are persons who are content to vibrate and work on the single digit pulsation and put their talents to excellent use in that position rather than try for the esoteric vibration of the Master Numbers. This depends a lot on other numbers which concern several other categories in numerology.

The main purpose of finding your DESTINY NUMBER is to realize where you are in life's stream and learn to flow with it.

The DESTINY NUMBER and your BIRTH SIGN are two things that you cannot change. You were born on a certain day, month, and year, for you chose to be here at that time to experience what you have come to this lifetime to learn.

Another way to research and discover if you have a hidden Master Number is to add this way:

February 24, 1928 = 2 + 6 + 19 + 28 = **55** or **1**
March 2, 1942 = 3 + 2 + 19 + 42 = **66** or **3**
March 3, 1940 = 3 + 3 + 19 + 40 = **66** or **3**

The following pages will interpret the number that you have chosen to go with your birth sign for this lifetime.

DESTINY NUMBER 1

This is one of the more ambitious signs of Pisces. This creative influence will open channels to your various talents. You have the possibility of bridging into the vibrations of any of the other zodiacal signs. For instance: do you want the freedom of thought that the Aquarian has, or the stubbornness of purpose that Taurus acts on? Study the birth signs to understand their vibrations and how people of certain signs act and react to situations. You can draw on the particular sign's vibrations to help you to make a decision. Remember that people of other signs and numbers are also reacting to their various experiences in life.

This is valuable information for all Pisces adventurers. There are bits and pieces of all the other signs residing in the Pisces house. So you can pick and choose your direction instead of reacting in an undecided manner. This makes an interesting game for you to play.

Develop a strength within yourself so that criticism intended to divert your attention from your goals does not get under your skin. Your personal integrity is acute, you are not really interested in maneuvering others to do what you want to do. You can get stuck on the point of indecision.

You need attention and encouragement to stay with your projects—projects that are full of imagination that can inspire others.

NEGATIVE: We sincerely hope you have not been invalidated in your childhood for your imaginative dreams. Your sensitivity can be crushed even as an adult. It may be a little hard to be out there on that newly discovered star; gets pretty lonely knowing that you are right and no one else can understand your visions of truth and beauty.

Number 1

Color: Red—for energy.
Element: Fire—more energy. Take your vitamins.
Musical Note: C—for the self-starter.

DESTINY NUMBER 2

You have planted the seeds of imagination and action in your former lifetimes, and in this life you have earned a rest. However, this time, Pisces, you have a lot to learn about relationships. This compassionate number combined with your compassionate birth sign could assist you to become (or you already are) a good counselor.

2s are called the peacemakers as they know how to put one and one together (1 + 1 = 2) to form an alliance of good will. Your cool-headed intuition can tune into the minds of warring factions and bring harmony into existence. All the time your mind is going click, click with ideas of how to present a program that would be acceptable to both parties.

You can be (or are) a great trouble shooter, able to solve both sides of a problem with your charm and disarming techniques. Your solutions to problems may be a little unusual, stretching the credulity of the participants, even eliciting humor in the situation. Then the opponents say, "Wait a minute, that's not so impossible," and everyone gets down to the business of settling the dispute.

Your mate or lover will appreciate your gentleness and charm (and the flowers, gifts and funny cards). Your sensitivity to their moods endears you to them.

You may not receive the awards and kudos of a 1, but you will know who is the power behind the throne. This knowledge is reward enough for you really do not want to be in the public eye unless you have other strong signs and numbers in your chart.

NEGATIVE: Impatience follows you all your life until you realize that waiting for others' decisions gives you more time to organize your thoughts and your rebuttals. You can become overly sensitive about your feelings and attribute general statements that are critical to be personal affronts.

Number 2

Color: Orange—for balance and harmony.
Element: Water—for emotions.
Musical Note: D—for harmony.

DESTINY NUMBER 3

You may have talents, Pisces, and tend to scatter your energies trying to discover which one to follow. It is a temptation to start several things at once and then decide that you need a vacation from all that hassle. Well, **3**s may be here on a vacation after all.

3 is a social number, entertaining, charming your friends and associates into giving you what you want. The problem is to make up your mind as to what you really want!

You have two ways to go (as usual) in your search for success in business. One way would be working for someone, or a company, who can outline the goals and routines for you. You will have your rebellious times but you would tend to acceed to their programs. The other way would be to take advantage of the assistance that successful people offer you in your artistic and idealistic pursuits. In either instance you can gain the goals you have visualized if you stay on the positive side of this number, Pisces.

There are many people in the entertainment field who carry this number. They know how to employ flamboyant gestures, coupling them with the emotional output necessary to TV, stage and movie careers.

Your mate or lover will constantly be pleased with your surprises of theatre tickets, long romantic drives, or reservations at the finest restaurants.

NEGATIVE: Guard against changing your mind too often, you could confuse your close associates. Using the energy of your opposite sign, Virgo, brings a more organized attitude. You can pick up the vibes of others and reflect their attitudes back to them, so, be careful about invalidating your boss or your mate. Don't waste your talents.

Number 3

Color: Yellow—for expression to the world.
Element: Fire—for energy to express.
Musical Note: *E*—for feeling.

DESTINY NUMBER 4

This number has a stabilizing affect on your birth sign, Pisces. It will keep you from vacillating in your decisions, as you tend to be more organized in your approach to life.

You can manifest what you want this time around. If you can visualize the creativity of **1**, the diplomacy of **2** and the energy wrapped up in **3**, all coming together in the **4**, then you can see what "manifesting" means. Use these energies when you are faced with a decision. You may have to count to four to remember that this time you can use diplomacy—another time you may want to use your creative energy and to heck with the diplomacy. Since you love to choose, this number could be fun for you, Pisces.

Another wonderful aspect of **4** is the healing potential you have in your hands. Esoterically you can work on the etheric body if you want to take the responsibility of this kind of magnetic healing.

Your mate or lover may be a little confused about an organized Piscean, so your little secret can remain yours, if you wish.

Your Neptune self is exhibiting the calm waters of a placid sea. Your Neptune self can also intuit the stormy waters ahead and be prepared for them. Your tendency is to retreat and dive deeply into your inner-most self for security reasons. When you intuit these stormy waters (or scenes) you can also hide behind the rock of stability, stating ideas and ideals.

NEGATIVE: Many people move slower mentally than you do, Pisces, so use a little patience to get along with them. While you can see several roads ahead, being Piscean, another **4** may only see one avenue of approach to success. Instead of invalidating the other person, use your charm and persuasion to get him on your side.

Number 4

Color: Beautiful, healing green.
Element: Earth—another stabilizing factor.
Musical Note: *F*—for construction, building.

DESTINY NUMBER 5

Travel, excitement, and new experiences which will contribute to your spiritual and emotional growth is inherent in this Destiny Number, Pisces. The travel can be physical, mental (in study) or even astral, if you are interested in the metaphysical side of life.

You could profit from these new adventures if you do not withdraw when too many choices come your way. As you seek life and become willing to try different approaches to your business or love life, you can make your dreams come true. You are the dreamer and visualizer!

5s do not stand still in the backwash of life. They usually pursue life with vigor, knowing that seeking adventure may succeed or it may not turn out the way they envisioned it. What the heck—it is still an adventure! Sometimes the anticipation is more thrilling than the success. When we reach our goals it sometimes seems like the end of an era, and this can be a let down.

This is a sensual number, relating experiences to the touching, loving and feeling part of you. This reveals the artistic side of you, Pisces, for you appreciate good music and elevated conversation.

This is also the number of creative mind, taking the 1's original idea and changing it into something else or even something better than the original. Many improved inventions have come through 5s.

NEGATIVE: The sensual part of 5 can increase your intake of food, drink or drugs, so it is something to be a little careful about. Fear of change is the essence of this number, fear of trying anything new and different. The "essence of life" is negated if you do not take advantage of this exciting number, Pisces.

Number 5

Color: Turquoise—like a refreshing breeze.
Element: Air—the breath of life.
Musical Note: G—denoting changeableness.

DESTINY NUMBER 6

This number is a radiation of harmony, Pisces. You really are not interested in fighting, chaos, things that do not work (like people) and carelessness. This harmonious number brings you the power of logic so you can adjust to the problems and challenges in this lifetime.

Any profession or job where you can be of service to people would be compatible with this number; like social service, teacher, physician, personnel work or professional guardian. In your concern for justice you would make a good judge, defense attorney, or statesman. You seek facts, not rumors, then carefully analyze both sides of the argument in order to exercise your inner wisdom. You would also do well as a dramatic actor or a musician. Look at all those talents, Pisces!

6s like home and family. They create order and insist on it. Their interest in food goes beyond mere eating, for they like to create exotic dishes. Their mate or lover can just turn over the kitchen to the male or female Piscean and read the evening paper while Pisces putters with the pots and pans.

You take good care of your money as you do your loved ones, so your mate never has to worry about you hiding from work. It isn't that you like work, you just know this is the way to get what you want out of life. If you have an expensive hobby you know you have to work for it.

NEGATIVE: In your concern for justice be careful you do not meddle in other people's affairs when you are not invited. Sometimes your feeling of always being right (when you are in a good mood) could be misconstrued by friends and business associates as an ego trip. Not so. You have carefully weighed the pros and cons before you make a clear-cut decision.

Number 6

Color: Royal blue—for stability.
Element: Earth—for responsibility.
Musical Note: A—for receptivity.

DESTINY NUMBER 7

You have always wanted to be free, Pisces, and this number (handled on the positive side) does free you to make your own choices. This does not make it any easier, as making a choice is difficult for you; however, the freedom to do it yourself (now that you know this) does enlarge your space to operate. No one is going to hamper you from achieving your goals unless you let them.

You don't even have to have goals because this number frees you from your past and lets you move into the future with confidence. It is like crossing a bridge, you see this side and the other and you want to cross this stream. Sometimes the planks on the bridge are rotten so you need to get some new boards to make it safe for yourself by building a new bridge (of consciousness).

7 is also called the "eye of the needle," seeing from this dimension to another with ease. 7 is analytical, looking at the past to see where your successes and mistakes were, then looking to the future to see how you can do better. When you have this number in any of the numerology categories you need to stop and take a look at what you are doing. You can unstick yourself from habit, from doing things in the same old way, and from your old attitudes.

Your mate or lover will find that you are exciting to live with. Living with you will never be dull! A stable 4 or 8 will keep you grounded or provide grounding for your freedom.

NEGATIVE: You can become skeptical of your own abilities, Pisces, and withdraw from the fray. If you become too confused you might try blaming others, even though you know this doesn't work. The compassionate Pisces will bring you up rather short if you try it. At the lowest level of negativity you can become suppressive to others, stopping them from doing what THEY want to do.

Number 7

Color: Violet—for reverence.
Element: Water—for reflection on the issues.
Musical Note: *B*—for reflection on self.

DESTINY NUMBER 8

This is one of the most powerful numbers in numerology, Pisces. It represents primal energy, the power to achieve success on a material level. When a Piscean decides to win he no longer impersonates the dual fishes who are undecided on which direction to swim; he becomes the whale ploughing through calm or turbulent waters to achieve a goal. With this number there is no stopping you, Pisces, if you decide to take advantage of this vibration.

You can become (or are) the leader and director of a business or several businesses, handling the money situation with ease. 8 is power, money and prosperity on the positive side.

Occupations which require physical stamina would be more appealing to you. You find release in the exercise of your physical muscles, thus sports, yoga, athletic competition and sports car racing would be examples of the outpouring of your physical energies.

Your spiritual side can be opened also as 8 gives you the opportunity to open your third eye and experience seeing auras, seeing visions of the future and opening the channels to spiritual energy.

Your mate or lover will need to recognize your desire to succeed. You will always have a good home and an ample bank account if you stay on the positive side of this number, Pisces.

NEGATIVE: This is the love of money, power and glory which destroys by climbing over others in your rise to the top; ignoring the "little people" to gain your objectives. This is impatience to get your own way, plotting and scheming to get ahead. As an 8, Pisces, you can get ahead without resorting to negative force.

NUMBER 8

Color: Rose—the color of love.
Element: Earth—for achievement, material gain or esoteric enlightenment.
Musical Note: High C—for research into the intuitive esoteric world.

DESTINY NUMBER 9

This is a good number for you, Pisces, as it represents love for all mankind. **9**s are the servers of mankind, the ones who go out on the highways and byways to bring the sheep into the fold.

You would make a good evangelist, speaker, or volunteer in charitable fund-raising efforts. This is brotherly love, recognizing that all persons have unique experiences which compel them to act as they do. This all-encompassing love can spread out to all those you meet and inspire them to act in love and compassion for their fellow man (or woman).

Your emotional attachments to individuals may be short, but intense, as you move from one person to another. These intense relationships may bring frustration to others but in time they realize you do not want to possess them. You inspire and set them free.

Your destiny is working in the mainstream of life where you can be an instrument for good—social worker, reformer, rehabilitation worker, healer, defense attorney, or nutritionist. Any occupation that serves the populace would be good for you. Even dramatics and singing would bring your love to your audiences.

This is also the number of a person who gets things together from start to finish. Finish your cycles of action, jobs and tasks. This ability to finish a job can lead you on to advancement in your chosen profession. Many people start many things but few complete their tasks.

NEGATIVE: You may find that you are being drained of your energies since you spread yourself too thin over many projects. Your mental side says it can be done, and your emotional side says, "Help." Watch your financial resources also; your kindliness can drain your pocketbook.

Number **9**

Color: Yellow-gold—for perfection.
Element: Fire—for warmth.
Musical Note: High *D*—for accomplishment.

DESTINY NUMBER 11

This is the first MASTER NUMBER after all the single digits from 1 through **9**. Master Numbers carry a responsibility for they are higher vibrations of the single digit they reduce to. For example: **11** = 1 + 1 = **2**. So **11** should be correctly written **11/2** to show that a person could be vibrating on either or both levels. This holds true for all the other Master Numbers.

This is the number of the perfectionist, your intuition can develop to a genius level, Pisces. Your search for truth can raise your level of intelligence, as well as that of others, if you desire to share your knowledge with them.

Sometimes **11s** are reluctant to reveal what they know since they feel that "everyone" knows about that. Try sharing some of your knowledge with people who are interested in the same things you are and you will be surprised how much more you know. You may also discover new ways to examine your way of life, your job, your mate or your family by exchanging ideas.

Share and exchange knowledge and feelings with whom it may concern to bring a better understanding between you and those who are important to you, Pisces.

You will receive flashes of illumination which could light up the path for many to follow. Your perceptions of a perfect world could influence those around you. We always hope that this is for good.

NEGATIVE: Since you are intuitively brilliant and your goals are inspiring you will draw many people to you. This could overwhelm and trap you for many geniuses become self-superior and fanatical about their mission in life. On the other hand, you could keep all these wonderful discoveries to yourself, thereby enriching no one.

Number 11

Color: Silver—this is for attraction. You can magnetize people to your side and support.
Element: Air—for the idealist who builds dream castles—don't knock it—it all starts with a dream.
Musical Note: High E—for magnetism.

DESTINY NUMBER 22

You are destined to become the head of a corporation, a big business, or take a high government position or in general use your talents in a practical universal way. You have a responsibility to the times and the tides in the affairs of men (and women). You can achieve recognition on a worldwide scale as you make contributions to society.

You need to think big and act big as you seek out the giants of industry who will further your plans. Get in contact with those in power and take your place alongside them. As a Piscean, the compassionate one, you can facilitate the rebuilding of a good world, instead of a repressive one.

You can be a forceful speaker for your dynamic aura encompasses the audience. You also receive a sort of radar from the audience which helps make a strong line of communication between you and them.

Investigate law, commerce, communications (such as TV and radio) and politics to achieve your dreams.

Your mate or lover will enjoy your romantic approach as well as dinner at the finest restaurants, expensive but appropriate gifts and your undivided attention at the proper times. You need a mate or lover who is aware of your tremendous power.

NEGATIVE: If you cannot follow through with your grandiose schemes you will be known as the big talker not the big doer. Also, if you do not strive to reach farther than the average person, you may become frustrated, involved in petty works and details. On the lowest vibration, this is crime on a large scale.

Number 22

> Color: Red-gold—for practical wisdom. Use the things you have learned for practical application rather than fantasies.
> Element: Water—for cleansing. Wash away your doubts and see your path clearly.
> Musical Note: High F—for physical mastery.

DESTINY NUMBER 33

This is the Master Number of emotional mastery. This is the ability to learn (unless you already know) about the emotions and how to use them to better understanding, Pisces.

Your ruler Neptune and the mutable water sign of your birth connects to the emotions. **33** gives you the possibility of bringing all these factors together and under control. Then you can use this knowledge for your own enlightenment as well as using it in a proper way (surely) to enlighten others.

Think of **33** as being the combination of **11**, the perfectionist, and **22**, the physical master who can put your dreams and visions into material form. Use your intuition or "feelings" to go about doing this or that. Your flashes of intuition will carry emotion with them, which helps to set this information in your mind. Sometimes flashes of intuition are just that, and they disappear as quickly as they appear unless there is feeling in them.

22 knows that the plan can materialize and be perfect if effort is applied in the right direction. Realizing this, a **33** can bring a balance to disagreements by using humor to release the tension. All levels of emotion are useful at different times—even anger. We suggest that the emotions not be used to hurt or avenge anyone.

Your mate or lover is going to enjoy your company to the utmost, Pisces. You are the gentle or fiery lover, depending on your mood.

NEGATIVE: The trap of this number is trying to control other people through their emotions, getting them angry so they lose control, or frustrating them so they become angry and make mistakes. This, of course, will reflect on you at a later date. Be particular in your choices of goals, for you can sway people through their emotions.

Number **33**

Color: Deep sky-blue—for intensity.
Element: Water—for emotional mastery.
Musical Note: High G—for emotional healing.

DESTINY NUMBER 44

If you thought **8** was powerful, take a good look at this number and see what it brings, Pisces. This is double power to manifest what you want on the material plane. This is the mental master who can visualize, analyze and then materialize his dreams and aspirations.

The MIND is a complex structure containing receptors (the way we see and perceive things), reactors (the way we react to different stimuli), and analytical functions. The mental master uses the latter part of the mind, the analytical portion that uses logic to determine the answers to challenges and problems. You can approach a challenge through the analytical doorway, look at the facts, then use your inherent intuitional abilities to dissect the certainties and the uncertainties until you arrive at a conclusion. This is analogous to two related things like the picture of a completed jigsaw and a pile of jigsaw pieces. How do you logically solve this puzzle? By fitting the correct pieces together.

Think of **44** as being a combination of **11**, the idealist, and **33**, the emotional master, and you get a little different twist. **44** would then arrive at the solution through vision and feeling. You would be using your intuitional ability to perfect your project.

Your mate or lover needs to understand this tremendous power that moves you in several directions. There is tenderness and passion here—what a nice combination.

NEGATIVE: If you try to control people through mental cruelty it will backfire on you. Invalidating others—not listening to their side of the story—refusing to compromise—is a negative manifestation of your energy.

Number **44**

Color: Blue-green—for tranquility and healing. This color calms the intense fire of ambition so that it can be directed into proper channels.
Element: Earth—representing mental mastery.
Musical Note: High A—for mental healing of self and others.

DESTINY NUMBER 55

As light from the sun beams down to the earth, breaking through the prism of consciousness to become warmth, intelligence and tranquility, so does a **55** (if willing) act as a prism to bring understanding to us from higher dimensions.

Think of **55** as being a combination of **22**, the physical master, and **33**, the emotional master. Added together you become the practical master of things on this plane of existence and are working to conquer your emotions to bring a moving life force into action. This life energy can elevate your own consciousness as well as others.

Or think of **55** as being a combination of **11** and **44** wherein the dreamer designs a world of his own and is able to see it take place on this third dimension. This is the architect who designs beautiful structures and oversees the construction, seeing his drawings come to life. We can become (or are) architects of our own lives. We put life into the way we truly want things to be. Think about it. We can put energy into sickness as well as wellness.

If you follow this course you will be admired for your tenacity, your creativity and your personal integrity, Pisces.

NEGATIVE: It's a little lonely on this high pinnacle of endeavor, Pisces. If you choose the negative side of this number you are karma burdened with inaction on the right path. This is where victims of life are still walking in darkness, seeing no light or path. Choose to look forward in a positive manner instead of wallowing in self-pity.

Number 55

Color: Red-violet—the abundant life energy. Let this life force flow out to all those around you, Pisces.
Element: Air—for spirituality. Discover the way of the masters. Meditate.
Musical Note: Chord of G—for spiritual healing.

DESTINY NUMBER 66

This is a powerful number, Pisces, and can be found through the Research and Discovery method, page 26—try it. This number radiates love energy; it is a Master Number which carries a lot of power in and with love. This love extends from self to others, Pisces, knowing that you cannot love others unless you know and recognize the perfection of your own soul.

This is not an ego trip; it is a full realization of outpouring love through the acceptance of karma-free relationship in soul. The inner self receives a vision of perfection and yearns for this love relationship with the soulmate and the supreme being.

You can seesaw between the Master Number **66** and **3**, which is its reduction. Sometimes you feel love and sometimes you just want to entertain people with humor and compassion.

66 is truly the cosmic mother, whether you are a male or female, the double 6 leading to the 9 ($6 \times 6 = 36$; $3 + 6 = $ **9**), brotherly love.

You are here to keep the love flame going and we do not necessarily mean the sex act, although that is an important part of lovingness. We are speaking of the love and joy in the total universe.

NEGATIVE: The higher the vibration, the lower a person can sink if he acts on the negative side of the Master Numbers. This number can be used as a tool to enslave others, having them do things "in love" that go against your moral sense. Love also can be withheld as punishment or through anger at another person. This love can become selfish, possessive and jealous of lovers and friends.

Number **66**

Color: Ultra-rose—meditation on this color will open the heart chakra more fully.

Element: Fire—for burning away the dross, the contempt, the frustration, the hate, and bringing forth the imprisoned love for self and others.

Musical Note: Any chord struck in harmony—bringing the soul in balance. Find the particular chord to which you vibrate.

YOUR PERSONAL CHART

Birthdate _____

Birth Number_____

Birth Sign_____

Birth Element_____

This planetary aspect represents the moral excellence and goodness that the soul has achieved in former lifetimes, virtues which will assist a person in this lifetime.

Birth Musical Note_____

Personal Year for 1991_____

Personal Year for 1992_____

Personal Year for 1993_____

Personal Year for 1994_____

Personal Year for 1995_____

Personal Year for 1996_____

Personal Year for 1997_____

Personal Year for 1998_____

Personal Month Numbers:

January _____   July_____

February _____   August _____

March _____   September_____

April _____   October_____

May _____   November_____

June _____   December_____

Challenges:

Major_____

1st Sub-challenge_____

2nd Sub-challenge_____

PERSONAL YEAR

The PERSONAL YEAR NUMBER is the vibration that influences your life in any given year. This is a fine focus of JUPITER, the planet of benevolence and idealism. Jupiter showers you with all the good things of life as long as you recognize what the good things are. If you are operating on the negative side of Jupiter, it could lead you into extravagance and greediness.

To obtain this number you add your BIRTH MONTH and your BIRTH DAY to the year you are seeking. For example: If your birth date is March 17, 1939, and you want to find the PERSONAL YEAR for 1981 you do this:

Add 3 (March) to 17 (the day) to 1981 = 2001; then add 2001 (2 + 0 + 0 + 1) = **3**. So **3** is the PERSONAL YEAR for the year 1981 for the person with the birth date of March 17, 1939.

Do not use your own birth year; use the year in which you wish to find your PERSONAL YEAR.

PERSONAL MONTH

Still under the influence of that great planet, JUPITER, we also find our own PERSONAL MONTH by adding our PERSONAL YEAR to the current month or the month we are seeking.

Example: March 17, 1939 is the birth date. We want to find the PERSONAL MONTH for May 1981. Since we have already established the PERSONAL YEAR for this birth date for 1981 as **3**, we simply take the **3** and add it to the month of May, which is represented by **5**.

3 (Personal Year) + **5** (May) = **8** PERSONAL MONTH.

Compute your PERSONAL MONTHS and find the interpretations on the following pages.

TABLE OF PERSONAL MONTHS

*JUPITER: EXPANSION,   UNDERSTANDING,   FRIENDLINESS,
ABUNDANCE, INSPIRATION, INCREASE, SPUR.*

The definitive words for Jupiter listed above captured the essence
of the positive side of Jupiter's vibrations. Understand these
words by using a good dictionary as you discover the true meaning for yourself. Meditating on all the descriptive words given in
this booklet will assist you also.

The NEGATIVE side of the JUPITER vibration is:
EXTRAVAGANCE, INDULGENCE, CYNICISM, GREED.

When we talk about the TIMING of your decisions we need to
remember that Jupiter has an influence as well as the vibration of
the number that you find for your own PERSONAL MONTH. The
interpretations for personal months are as follows:

PERSONAL MONTH 1

This is a time for action, a time to seek new, exciting offers which
could enhance your position in your profession, in your relationships with your mate, or with your family. Your search for
wellness for your physical, mental, or spiritual body is inspired by
this number. Be sure to check how this agrees with your Destiny
Number and your Personal Year Number. Understanding these
three categories will help you to understand yourself. Use the
water sign to cool down rising tempers at injustices to yourself.
Welcome opportunities that come your way, you have the ability
to change them to suit yourself. These changes could mean a new
job, a change of residence or a change of attitude toward your
life. When you get ready to blast ahead nothing can stop you,
Pisces!

NEGATIVE: You could become bossy and arrogant over your successes or your mistakes, thereby incurring the wrath of your
associates. Watch it.

PERSONAL MONTH 2

This is the month to take a good look at the friends you have, see where they are headed and if you want to continue the relationship, Pisces. Sometimes we follow our peer group through inertia. It is just easier to not resist. However, you have an intelligent mind geared to imaginative projects and products. Good relationships can be formed this month if your Destiny Number is compatible. Always look at your Personal Year and your Destiny Number to understand the vibrations of each month. Small issues may assume exaggerated importance this month, so delay any important decisions until next month. You will be ready to move ahead with your plans that you are formulating this month.

NEGATIVE: Your observation of another's motives may get you down. You may indulge in fantasies about how you are being "treated." Then you drop into the "poor me's" and your glum exterior drives people from your presence.

PERSONAL MONTH 3

Good relationships can be formed this month also, but from a different perspective—that of charm. You can charm your way into another's heart. Have a good time this month, Pisces. Relax and let go. This is vacation time for your mind and body. Don't be too concerned about the past or future, you are here now, not there. Laughter cures a lot of ills and we all are more serious than we need to be. Communicate good fun to others and it will lift your spirits also. Listen to what people are really saying, Pisces, you may be assuming too much by half-listening. On the esoteric side, meditating to bring in knowledge from higher beings is compatible with this number. Experiment and experience.

NEGATIVE: You could be jumping around from job to job (in your mind) and never settle on any one. Intolerance raises its ugly head as you judge other people for their inconsistency. In your successes you could become conceited and exaggerate your importance.

PERSONAL MONTH 4

When you make up your mind, Pisces, you come up with some splendid ideas. **4**, wherever it occurs in your chart, is the number of organization, getting your act together. This month you will need a lot of patience to sort through the tasks to find the ones which need your immeditate attention. Rather than waste your time deciding which of these tasks takes priority, just choose one, do it and go to the next. Indecision just builds a higher wall to getting the job done. Most of the fear of decision is the fear of making a mistake because this would destroy your self-image. Other people realize that perfection is hard to come by, Pisces. Use your practical, intelligent side to build toward the future. All considerations toward your work, hobbies, and family must be given careful thought; next month you can move ahead with the choice you have made.

NEGATIVE: You can become so engrossed with making all the choices that you forget that others around you have wishes also. You can become rigid in your opinions, refusing to even speculate on another way of doing some task. Relax a little, Pisces.

PERSONAL MONTH 5

Now is your chance to move into situations that you have planned. The force (vibration) is with you as they say in the movie *Star Wars*. This is a time of activity; you have remained grounded too long in your present occupation and need a new outlook. You may even see your work from a different perspective. This is a changeable month. You will be meeting new people, looking at new concepts with your vivid imagination. There is also travel. This does not mean that you *have* to travel, just that it is a good month to do it. Maybe it is good for you because your luggage will arrive at the same place and time you do!

NEGATIVE: You can become very restless, wondering why (you wonder a lot) you were so together last month and this month things just sort of fell apart.

PERSONAL MONTH 6

This is the month to center your attentions on love for your mate, lover, and family. This love moves outward to encompass them; they sense your inner peace. It may take a lot of patience for you to face their shortcomings, to listen to their problems, yet you have an inner ear that can hear the underlying cry for help. This is a personal time for you to listen to inner guidance on what to do, Pisces. What is happening can't all be bad or coming from outside yourself. Perhaps your attitude needs changing. When you are helping others you do not need to take on their burdens; you only need to listen to the real problem and then turn it into an asset with love. Protect those who need your calm assurance. Bring yourself into balance by reaching for love in your meditative period.

NEGATIVE: You could become so absorbed in others' problems that you interfere. The caution is to listen—not advise. Sometimes we want to help so much we turn people off with our offer of assistance.

PERSONAL MONTH 7

You will not be bored this month, Pisces, because there are so many mysteries for you to unravel. There are many authorities on many subjects and the information becomes confusing. Your inner wisdom will lead you to the right choices if you will listen to your inner guidance this month. Being positive or looking on the bright side brings better vibrations than being negative about what is happening around you. This is the time to reflect on things undone, analyze and plan how you can reach your goals. Be ready to move. You can close the gap between wishing for something and actually realizing it.

NEGATIVE: Your intelligent mind seeks peace and comfort, so you can get confused with all the chaos going on around you. You may want to tear down another's dreams and hopes for a better life.

PERSONAL MONTH 8

Take a good look at your money situation this month, Pisces, to see if you have the opportunity to increase your prosperity in some way. You might have to work more hours, collect that which is due you, or go after a promotion. You can do this when you set your mind to it. Sometimes the easy way of keeping the peace and letting things slide just doesn't work. This month brings rewards for past efforts. Think about your goals, where do you really want to end up? We know that you are not that interested in becoming a millionaire, but money and power is nice to have for a while. "The tides in the affairs taken at the flood leads on to fortune," says Shakespeare, and they will release a lot of good things for you, Pisces. If you have everything you want and are interested in the metaphysical world, you can open or reopen your third eye by a direct application of meditation and your energy this month.

NEGATIVE: Money and power could slip through your fingers if you ignore this positive vibration and scatter your energies in aimless pursuits.

PERSONAL MONTH 9

Look around you and see the material things you no longer need, and how they clutter your life. Take them to a swap meet, or have a garage sale. It is a little emotional to let go of souvenirs and things to which we have become attached—yet this is inhibiting your growth. Next month you can start fresh with lots of room to store your new purchases. This is also a good time to do some service for mankind. Do some charity work or something for your friends. Express your love for your mate by bringing gifts and unusual treats home. Love and share your thoughts and goals so that communication is smoothed out.

NEGATIVE: You could be rushing forward, leading the band of do-gooders only to find yourself alone with no one behind you. Watch how your emotions can inspire you—not perspire you.

CHALLENGES OF LIFE

CHALLENGES are obstacles we encounter during this lifetime. We are now concerned with the timing of events that stop you from progressing until you understand just what the obstacle is and means.

In the FIRST HALF of your lifetime, you will encounter a SUB or minor challenge which is represented by a number.

In the SECOND HALF of your lifetime, you will encounter a SUB or minor challenge which is represented by a number.

The MAJOR CHALLENGE, also represented by a number, is with you your entire lifetime until you solve the mystery. We accepted these challenges when we decided to incarnate on this planet so that we can strengthen the weak links in our destiny. Recognizing these weak links by finding the negative influences of these numbers will be helpful.

SATURN is the planet known as the DISCIPLINARIAN, the teacher, the door to the initiation and all these good things we shy away from or fear. See Saturn's other side—if you have no game going, no challenge and life proceeds smoothly straight down the road with the same scenery—where is the spice? Understand the good that Saturn brings us. Saturn is connected to the challenges of life.

FIRST SUB CHALLENGE: Subtract the number of your birth MONTH from the number of your birth DAY or vice versa.

SECOND SUB CHALLENGE: Subtract the number of your birth DAY from your reduced birth YEAR or vice versa.

MAJOR CHALLENGE: Subtract the FIRST SUB CHALLENGE from the SECOND SUB CHALLENGE or vice versa. Place all these numbers in your PERSONAL CHART on page 26.

EXAMPLE: March   17, 1939
            3   8   4
          ─────────────────
                 5   4   = **5** is the First Sub Challenge
                 1   **4** is the Second Sub Challenge
                             1 is the Major Challenge

TABLE OF CHALLENGES

1—Many people will try to dominate and control your life. The remedy is choosing your own way without being belligerent about it. Know when you are right and please yourself after considering all the facts. Strengthen your self-determinism and be the daring, creative person you really are. Dependence on others can limit your talents.

2—Your feelings are uppermost and you are apt to turn others' opinions into personal affronts. This sensitivity can be very useful if you "tune" into people and see where they are. Cultivate a broader outlook on life and learn to be cooperative without being indecisive. Be thoughtful and consider the welfare of others as well as your own.

3—Social interaction frightens you and your reaction is to withdraw or become the loud overreactor. Each violent swing of the pendulum suggests that you are living in a personal construct without reality. Develop your sense of humor; try painting, dancing, writing or any artistic sort of self-expression that can bring out the real you.

4—This easy challenge is LAZINESS! However it can lead you into a rut where it is too much trouble to get out of that comfortable chair to answer the phone. Finish your cycles of activity and you will find your energy level rising. The other side of this challenge is rigidity. Learn patience and tolerance without becoming a slave.

5—This "freedom" number allows us to progress BUT it does not mean doing anything and everything we desire without paying attention to our responsibilities. There are laws of society and universe that tell us to use moderation, not overindulgence, in sex, drugs, alcohol or food. Organize your life. Recognize duties to family and friends.

6—This idealistic number may lead you into thinking that you have the best of all possible answers and belief systems. Your opinions can be dogmatic where personal relationships are at the crossroads. Do not impose your "perfection" on others. Give will-

ingly of your time and knowledge without suppressing others'
creativity. Turn "smug" into "hug."

7—This research and discovery number challenges you to become
scientific and analytical. Heed your inner guidance. Develop a
patience with existing conditions and make an effort to improve
them. Do not stifle your spiritual nature. Your limitations are self-
imposed. Cultivate faith in the justice of the general plan of things
then seek to better it.

8—Wastefulness is the keyword for 8. This can be brought about by
carelessness or miserliness. A false sense of values, efficiency and
judgements can become fetishes in the material world. Use your
energies to cultivate good human relationships and avoid greed.
Be guided by reason and not by avarice. Honor, glory, fame and
money are okay if acquired in the right way.

9—This challenge is rare since it carries the lack of emotion and
human compassion. It also means judging others and refusing to
understand them because of an inflated ego. The time has come
for this person to learn to love and empathize with others.

0—Here is NO or ALL challenges. Study all the NUMBERS above
and see if you react to one. You have reached a point in your
spiritual development where you can choose which challenge to
release. Smooth the edges, learn and know the vibrations of the
independence of 1; the diplomat of 2; the emotional thrust of 3; the
diligence of 4; the expansion of 5; the adjustment of 6; the wisdom
of 7; the power of 8; and the Universal Brotherhood of 9.

If your CHALLENGES are the same as your DESTINY NUMBER,
give it very close scrutiny.

NUMBERS

Every number can be expressed on three levels—
POSITIVE—NEGATIVE—REPRESSIVE. This does not mean that a
person is expressing on all three levels. You can evaluate yourself
by observing:

1. How you react in certain situations.
2. What is your chronic emotional tone?
   Happy, grumpy, short-tempered, enthusiastic,
   fearful, bored, etc.?
3. Check how the interpretations listed below
   represent your over-all response to your daily grind.

POSITIVE	NEGATIVE	REPRESSIVE
Certain	Apathetic	Despotic
Enthusiastic	Unsure	Tyrannical
Definite	Antagonistic	Suppressive
Specific	Vacillating	Hostile
Searching	Non-feeling	Violent
Transforming	Covert	Stop Motions
Activating	Resentful	Hateful

This is the reason that people with the same numbers react
differently to certain situations and differ in attitude towards
themselves and others. You can choose which level you are now
on and change your level if you wish to change yourself. You can
also change your name or a few letters of your name to bring in
the vibrations of your choice.

See our book on Name Analysis—POTENTIAL! This book
gives you an in-depth analysis of your personality. It is soon to be
available at book stores or can be ordered direct from the Rices.

Number 1:
POSITIVE: Creative; optimistic; self-determined; creative mind
through feeling; can reach a higher dimension of awareness when
preceded by a 10.
NEGATIVE: Indecisive; arrogant; fabricator.
REPRESSIVE: Tyrannical; hostile; ill-willed.

Number **2**:
POSITIVE: Sensitive; rhythmic; patient; a lover; restful; a peacemaker; skilled; responsive to emotional appeal with love; protective.
NEGATIVE: Impatient; cowardly, overly sensitive.
REPRESSIVE: Mischievous; self-deluded; hostile.

Number **3**:
POSITIVE: Communicative; entertaining; charming; can acquire knowledge from higher beings; inspirational; an intuitive counselor.
NEGATIVE: Conceited; exaggerating; dabbling but never really learning anything exactly; gossiping.
REPRESSIVE: Hypocritical; intolerant; jealous.

Number **4**:
POSITIVE: Organizer; devoted to duty; orderly; loyal; able to heal etheric body by magnetism; works on higher levels; endures.
NEGATIVE: Inflexible; plodder; penurious; stiff; clumsy; rigid; argumentative.
REPRESSIVE: Hateful; suppressive; gets even.

Number **5**:
POSITIVE: Adventurous; understanding; clever; knows the essence of life; creative mind on the mental level; traveler; creative healer.
NEGATIVE: Inconsistency; self-indulgence; sloppy; tasteless; inelegant.
REPRESSIVE: Perverted; afraid of change; indulgence in drink, food, dope; no sympathy.

Number **6**:
POSITIVE: Harmonious; good judgement; love of home and family; balance; cosmic mother; self-realization; the doorway to higher mind through harmony.
NEGATIVE: Anxious; interfering; careless.
REPRESSIVE: Cynical; nasty; domestic tyranny.

Number **7**:
POSITIVE: Analytical; refined; studious; capable of inner wisdom; symbolizes the bridge from the mundane to the esoteric; the mystic; able to heal spiritual gaps.

NEGATIVE: Confused; skeptical; humiliates others; aloof; a contender.
REPRESSIVE: Malicious; a cheat; suppressive to self and others.

Number **8**:
POSITIVE: Powerful; a leader; director; chief; dependable; primal energy; can open third eye; money maker; sees auras.
NEGATIVE: Intolerant; biased; scheming; love of power—fame—glory without humility; impatient.
REPRESSIVE: Bigoted; abusive; oppressive; unjust.

Number **9**:
POSITIVE: Compassionate; charitable; romantic; aware; involved with the brotherhood of man; successful; finisher; merciful; humane.
NEGATIVE: Selfish; unkind; scornful; stingy; unforgiving; indiscreet; inconsiderate.
REPRESSIVE: Bitter; morose; dissipated; immoral.

Number **11**:   IDEALIST
POSITIVE: Idealistic; intuitive; cerebral; second sight; clairvoyant; perfection; spiritual; extrasensory perception; excellence; inner wisdom.
NEGATIVE: Fanatic; self-superiority; cynic; aimless; pragmatic; zealot.
REPRESSIVE: Dishonest; miserly; carnal; insolent.

Number **22**:   PHYSICAL MASTERY
POSITIVE: Universal power on the physical level; financier; cultured person; international direction in government; physical mastery over self.
NEGATIVE: Inferiority complex; indifference; big talker—not doer; inflated ego.
REPRESSIVE: Evil; viciousness; crime on a large scale; black magic.

Number **33**:   EMOTIONAL MASTERY
POSITIVE: The idealist with power to command or serve; leader who has emotions under control; constructive emotionally controlled ideas.
NEGATIVE: Erratic; useless; unemotional; not using his/her gifts of sensitivity to others.

REPRESSIVE: Power to work on other people's emotion to their detriment; riot leaders.

Number 44:   MENTAL MASTERY
POSITIVE: Universal builder with insight; can institute and assist world-wide reform for the good of mankind; can manifest his postulates.
NEGATIVE: Mental abilities used for confusion of worthwhile ideas; twists meanings of great statesmen and very able people for personal use.
REPRESSIVE: Crime through mental cruelty; uses mask of righteousness to do evil; psychotic.

Number 55:   LIFE ENERGY
POSITIVE: Abundant life; channels from higher dimensions with ease; brings light into existence; student of action; heals using life force.
NEGATIVE: Karma burdened with inaction on the right path; chooses to look backward and wallow in self-pity.
REPRESSIVE: Victim of life; in darkness; no path visible; withdraws; blames others.

Number 66:   LOVE ENERGY
POSITIVE: Self-realization through love; this love extends from self to others, knowing that one cannot love others unless one knows and recognizes the perfection of one's own soul.
NEGATIVE: Using love as a tool to enslave another; extreme selfishness and possessiveness; refusing love when time and person is correct.
REPRESSIVE: Seeing only the barriers to love; repressing loving attention to others; repressing the need to outpour cosmic love to others.

BIBLIOGRAPHY

Avery, K., *Numbers of Life*, Freeway Press
Bailey, A., *Esoteric Healing*, Lucis Pub. Co.
_____,*From Intellect to Intuition*, Lucis Pub. Co.
_____,*Initiation: Human and Solar*, Lucis Pub. Co.
_____,*Letters on Occult Meditation*, Lucis Pub. Co.
_____,*Problems of Humanity*, Lucis Pub. Co.
_____,*Telepathy*, Lucis Pub. Co.
Campbell, F., *Your Days are Numbered*, Gateway
Diegel, P., *Reincarnation and You*, Prism Pubs.
Fitzgerald, A., *Numbers for Lovers*, Manor Books
Johnson, V., & Wommack, T., *Secrets of Numbers*, Samuel
    Weiser, Inc.
Jordan, J., *Romance in Your Life*, DeVorss & Co.
_____,*Your Right Action Number*, DeVorss & Co.
Leek, S., *Magic of Numbers*, Collier-MacMillen, Pubs.
Long, M.F., *Growing into Light*, DeVorss & Co.
_____,*Huna Code in Religions*, DeVorss & Co.
_____,*Secret Science Behind Miracles*, DeVorss & Co.
_____,*Secret Science at Work*, DeVorss & Co.
_____,*Self Suggestion*, DeVorss & Co.
Lopez, V., *Numerology*, New American Library, Inc.
Rice, P. & V., *Potential! Name Analysis*, Samuel Weiser, Inc.
_____,*Timing*, F.A.C.E.
_____,*Triadic Communication*, F.A.C.E.
_____,*Thru the Numbers*, Samuel Weiser, Inc. (a series for each
    zodiac sign)
Roquemore, K.K. *It's All in Your Numbers*, Harper & Row
Schure, E., *Pythagoras and the Delphic Mysteries*,
    Health Research
Street, H., Taylor, A., *Numerology, its Facts and Secrets*,
    Wilshire Book Co.
Thommen, G. S., *Is this your Day?*, Crown Publishing Co.

YOUR PERSONAL CHART

Birthdate _____

Birth Number _____

Birth Sign _____

Birth Element _____

This planetary aspect represents the moral excellence and goodness that the soul has achieved in former lifetimes, virtues which
will assist a person in this lifetime.

Birth Musical Note _____

Personal Year for 1991 _____

Personal Year for 1992 _____

Personal Year for 1993 _____

Personal Year for 1994 _____

Personal Year for 1995 _____

Personal Year for 1996 _____

Personal Year for 1997 _____

Personal Year for 1998 _____

Personal Year for 1999 _____

Personal Year for 2000 _____

Personal Month Numbers:

January _____	July _____
February _____	August_____
March _____	September _____
April _____	October _____
May _____	November _____
June _____	December _____

Challenges:

Major _____

1st Sub-challenge _____

2nd Sub-challenge _____

YOUR PERSONAL CHART

Birthdate _____

Birth Number _____

Birth Sign _____

Birth Element _____

This planetary aspect represents the moral excellence and goodness that the soul has achieved in former lifetimes, virtues which
will assist a person in this lifetime.

Birth Musical Note _____

Personal Year for 1991 _____

Personal Year for 1992 _____

Personal Year for 1993 _____

Personal Year for 1994 _____

Personal Year for 1995 _____

Personal Year for 1996 _____

Personal Year for 1997 _____

Personal Year for 1998 _____

Personal Year for 1999 _____

Personal Year for 2000 _____

Personal Month Numbers:

    January _____   July _____

    February _____   August_____

    March _____   September _____

    April _____   October _____

    May _____   November _____

    June _____   December _____

Challenges:

    Major _____

    1st Sub-challenge _____

    2nd Sub-challenge _____

YOUR PERSONAL CHART

Birthdate _____

Birth Number _____

Birth Sign _____

Birth Element _____

This planetary aspect represents the moral excellence and goodness that the soul has achieved in former lifetimes, virtues which
will assist a person in this lifetime.

Birth Musical Note _____

Personal Year for 1991 _____

Personal Year for 1992 _____

Personal Year for 1993 _____

Personal Year for 1994 _____

Personal Year for 1995 _____

Personal Year for 1996 _____

Personal Year for 1997 _____

Personal Year for 1998 _____

Personal Year for 1999 _____

Personal Year for 2000 _____

Personal Month Numbers:

January _____		July _____	
February _____		August_____	
March _____		September _____	
April _____		October _____	
May _____		November _____	
June _____		December _____	

Challenges:

Major _____

1st Sub-challenge _____

2nd Sub-challenge _____

YOUR PERSONAL CHART

Birthdate _____

Birth Number _____

Birth Sign _____

Birth Element _____

This planetary aspect represents the moral excellence and goodness that the soul has achieved in former lifetimes, virtues which will assist a person in this lifetime.

Birth Musical Note _____

Personal Year for 1991 _____

Personal Year for 1992 _____

Personal Year for 1993 _____

Personal Year for 1994 _____

Personal Year for 1995 _____

Personal Year for 1996 _____

Personal Year for 1997 _____

Personal Year for 1998 _____

Personal Year for 1999 _____

Personal Year for 2000 _____

Personal Month Numbers:

January _____   July _____

February _____   August _____

March _____   September _____

April _____   October _____

May _____   November _____

June _____   December _____

Challenges:

Major _____

1st Sub-challenge _____

2nd Sub-challenge _____

YOUR PERSONAL CHART

Birthdate _____

Birth Number _____

Birth Sign _____

Birth Element _____

This planetary aspect represents the moral excellence and goodness that the soul has achieved in former lifetimes, virtues which
will assist a person in this lifetime.

Birth Musical Note _____

Personal Year for 1991 _____

Personal Year for 1992 _____

Personal Year for 1993 _____

Personal Year for 1994 _____

Personal Year for 1995 _____

Personal Year for 1996 _____

Personal Year for 1997 _____

Personal Year for 1998 _____

Personal Year for 1999 _____

Personal Year for 2000 _____

Personal Month Numbers:

January _____	July _____
February _____	August_____
March _____	September _____
April _____	October _____
May _____	November _____
June _____	December _____

Challenges:

Major _____

1st Sub-challenge _____

2nd Sub-challenge _____

YOUR PERSONAL CHART

Birthdate _____

Birth Number _____

Birth Sign _____

Birth Element _____

This planetary aspect represents the moral excellence and goodness that the soul has achieved in former lifetimes, virtues which
will assist a person in this lifetime.

Birth Musical Note _____

Personal Year for 1991 _____

Personal Year for 1992 _____

Personal Year for 1993 _____

Personal Year for 1994 _____

Personal Year for 1995 _____

Personal Year for 1996 _____

Personal Year for 1997 _____

Personal Year for 1998 _____

Personal Year for 1999 _____

Personal Year for 2000 _____

Personal Month Numbers:

January _____	July _____
February _____	August _____ _____
March _____	September _____
April _____	October _____
May _____	November _____
June _____	December _____

Challenges:

Major _____

1st Sub-challenge _____

2nd Sub-challenge _____

YOUR PERSONAL CHART

Birthdate _____

Birth Number _____

Birth Sign _____

Birth Element _____

This planetary aspect represents the moral excellence and goodness that the soul has achieved in former lifetimes, virtues which
will assist a person in this lifetime.

Birth Musical Note _____

Personal Year for 1991 _____

Personal Year for 1992 _____

Personal Year for 1993 _____

Personal Year for 1994 _____

Personal Year for 1995 _____

Personal Year for 1996 _____

Personal Year for 1997 _____

Personal Year for 1998 _____

Personal Year for 1999 _____

Personal Year for 2000 _____

Personal Month Numbers:

January _____	July _____
February _____	August_____
March _____	September _____
April _____	October _____
May _____	November_____
June _____	December _____

Challenges:

Major _____

1st Sub-challenge _____

2nd Sub-challenge _____

YOUR PERSONAL CHART

Birthdate _____

Birth Number _____

Birth Sign _____

Birth Element _____

This planetary aspect represents the moral excellence and goodness that the soul has achieved in former lifetimes, virtues which
will assist a person in this lifetime.

Birth Musical Note _____

Personal Year for 1991 _____

Personal Year for 1992 _____

Personal Year for 1993 _____

Personal Year for 1994 _____

Personal Year for 1995 _____

Personal Year for 1996 _____

Personal Year for 1997 _____

Personal Year for 1998 _____

Personal Year for 1999 _____

Personal Year for 2000 _____

Personal Month Numbers:

January _____   July _____

February _____   August_____

March _____   September _____

April _____   October _____

May _____   November _____

June _____   December _____

Challenges:

Major _____

1st Sub-challenge _____

2nd Sub-challenge _____

YOUR PERSONAL CHART

Birthdate _____

Birth Number _____

Birth Sign _____

Birth Element _____

This planetary aspect represents the moral excellence and goodness that the soul has achieved in former lifetimes, virtues which
will assist a person in this lifetime.

Birth Musical Note _____

Personal Year for 1991 _____

Personal Year for 1992 _____

Personal Year for 1993 _____

Personal Year for 1994 _____

Personal Year for 1995 _____

Personal Year for 1996 _____

Personal Year for 1997 _____

Personal Year for 1998 _____

Personal Year for 1999 _____

Personal Year for 2000 _____

Personal Month Numbers:

January _____   July _____

February _____   August _____

March _____   September _____

April _____   October _____

May _____   November _____

June _____   December _____

Challenges:

Major _____

1st Sub-challenge _____

2nd Sub-challenge _____

THE PRACTICAL PSYCHIC
John Friedlander & Cynthia Pearson

- Practical techniques for enlisting the •
resources of your own psychic ability

"How fascinating this book is—such a practical approach to the study of our nature that one wonders why no one has thought of doing it in just this way before!"
—Robert F. Butts, co-creator of the Seth books

"This book is spirited, spiritual and down-to-earth. The authors have done their homework—and a good deal more."
—Marilyn Ferguson, author of *The Aquarian Conspiracy*

"A wonderfully clear and inspiring book, full of valuable exercises and insights. The authors succeed in de-mystifying psychic work, making it accessible and empowering to the ordinary reader."
—Roger Woolger, Ph.D., author of *Other Lives, Other Selves*

John Friedlander, a graduate of Harvard Law School, channel, teacher and member of the original Jane Roberts/Seth classes teams up with Cynthia Pearson to teach psychic development. Step-by-step instructions are provided to help you unleash your psychic ability. You don't need to possess any special talents or abilities to be clairvoyant, telepathic, or precognitive. Read this book and bring your intuitive powers to life!

160 pp. • ISBN 0-87728-728-7 • Trade Paper, $9.95

"What's in a name?"
POTENTIAL
The Name Analysis Book
Paul and Valeta Rice

- Want to change your name?
- Or do you want to learn to live more comfortably with the one you've got?
- An easy-to-read guidebook that explains the universal meaning of your name.

Paul and Valeta Rice explore the depths of numerology to show you how your birth name holds the key to your inner self. They explain the numbers, master numbers and the special nuances of number combinations, so you can learn to analyze your name on many levels. Without having to know any complicated mathematical procedure, you will learn how to analyze:

- your desired self and dormant self
- your special abilities number
- your karmic number—and what you need to work on in this lifetime!
- the spiritual dimensions your name holds
- the layers of meaning you can derive from your name

With this book you will be able to discover what's in a name—and if you don't like the one you have, you can change it!

192 pp. ● ISBN 0-87728-632-9 ● Trade Paper, $8.95

WEISER ORDER FORM

Samuel Weiser, Inc.
Box 612, York Beach, Me 03910

You may use this form to order any of the Weiser publications listed in this book:

Title	Author	ISBN	Price

Shipping and handling: We ship UPS when possible so that lost shipments can be traced. Include $2.00 for orders under $10.00 and $3.00 for orders over $10.00.

Credit Card Orders: We accept MasterCard and Visa. Call to place your chargecard order: 1-800-423-7087.

☐ Please send me your free catalog.